POPULATION
Infographics

Chris Oxlade

Raintree

Raintree is an imprint of Capstone Global Library Limited, a company incorporated in England and Wales having its registered office at 7 Pilgrim Street, London, EC4V 6LB – Registered company number: 6695582

www.raintreepublishers.co.uk
myorders@raintreepublishers.co.uk

Edited by Rebecca Rissman, Dan Nunn, and John-Paul Wilkins
Designed by Philippa Jenkins
Original illustrations © Capstone Global Library Ltd 2014
Illustrations by HL Studios
Picture research by Elizabeth Alexander
Production by Vicki Fitzgerald
Originated by Capstone Global Library Ltd
Printed and bound in China

ISBN 978 1 406 27211 6
17 16 15 14 13
10 9 8 7 6 5 4 3 2 1

British Library Cataloguing in Publication Data
Oxlade, Chris.
Population. – (Infographics)
A full catalogue record for this book is available from the British Library.

Acknowledgements
We would like to thank the following for permission to reproduce photographs: Capstone Global Library p. 4; Shutterstock pp. 4 (© M.Stasy, © Pakhnyushcha, © Stella Caraman, © Thomas Bethge).

We would like to thank Diana Bentley and Marla Conn for their invaluable help in the preparation of this book.

Every effort has been made to contact copyright holders of any material reproduced in this book. Any omissions will be rectified in subsequent printings if notice is given to the publisher.

Disclaimer
All the internet addresses (URLs) given in this book were valid at the time of going to press. However, due to the dynamic nature of the internet, some addresses may have changed, or sites may have changed or ceased to exist since publication. While the author and publisher regret any inconvenience this may cause readers, no responsibility for any such changes can be accepted by either the author or the publisher.

CONTENTS

Some words are shown in bold, **like this**. You can find out what they mean by looking in the glossary.

ABOUT INFOGRAPHICS

An infographic is a picture that gives you information. Infographics can be graphs, charts, maps, or other sorts of pictures. The infographics in this book are about **population**.

Infographics make information easier to understand. We see infographics all over the place, every day. They appear in books, in newspapers, on the television, on websites, on posters, and in adverts.

Here's a simple infographic about how many people there are in the world.

World population

7.1 billion
people

7.1 billion
people would fill
860 cities like London

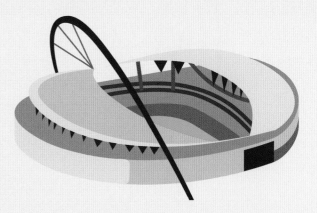

7.1 billion
people would fill
89,000 Olympic stadiums

WORLD POPULATION

The population of different continents

This map shows how many people live on each of the world's continents. Antarctica is not included as very few people live there!

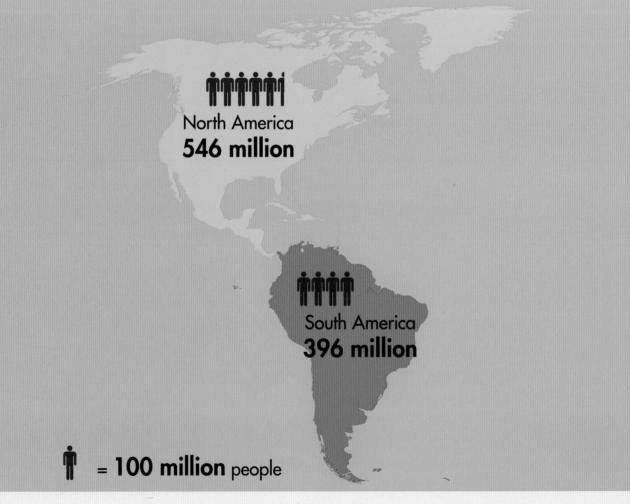

North America
546 million

South America
396 million

👤 = **100 million** people

Asia is by far
the most heavily
populated continent.

Europe
740 million

Asia
4.2 billion

Africa
1.1 billion

Oceania
37 million

The world's growing population

The growing planet Earth in this infographic shows how the world's **population** has grown in the last 1000 years.

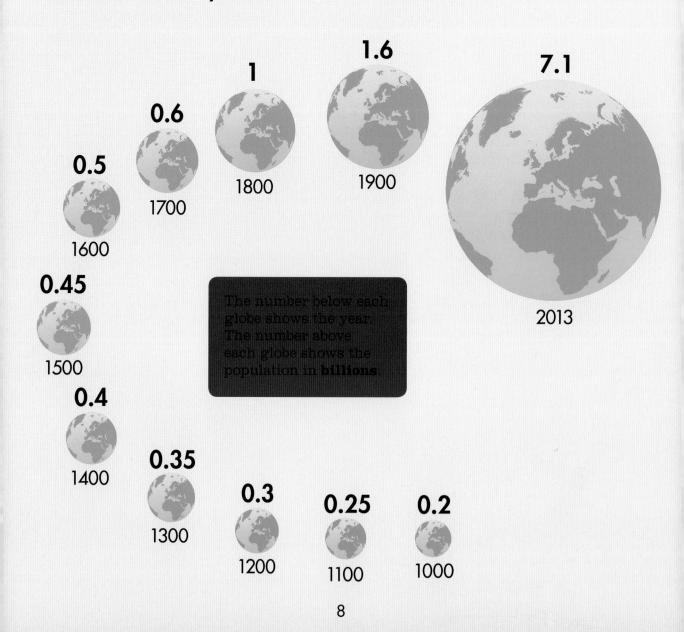

0.5
1600

0.6
1700

1
1800

1.6
1900

7.1
2013

0.45
1500

0.4
1400

0.35
1300

0.3
1200

0.25
1100

0.2
1000

The number below each globe shows the year. The number above each globe shows the population in **billions**.

The future population

The world's population is growing all the time. This chart shows how the world's population might grow by the year 2100.

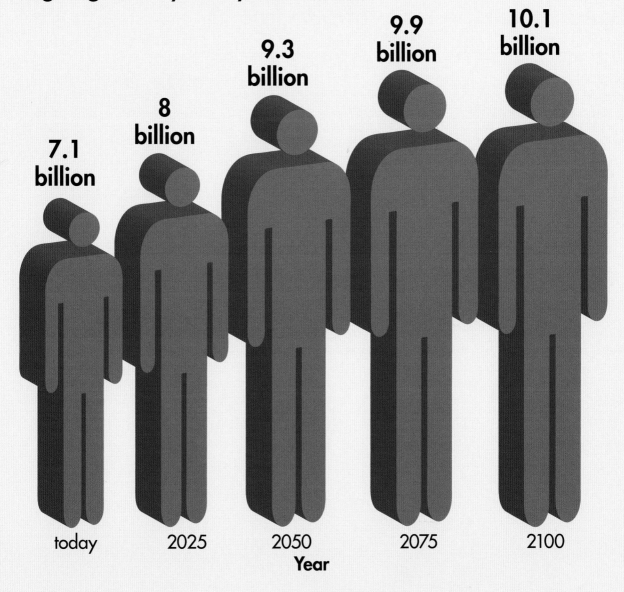

7.1 billion — today
8 billion — 2025
9.3 billion — 2050
9.9 billion — 2075
10.1 billion — 2100

Year

COUNTRIES AND CITIES

Countries with most people

This map shows the ten countries with the biggest **populations** in the world today.

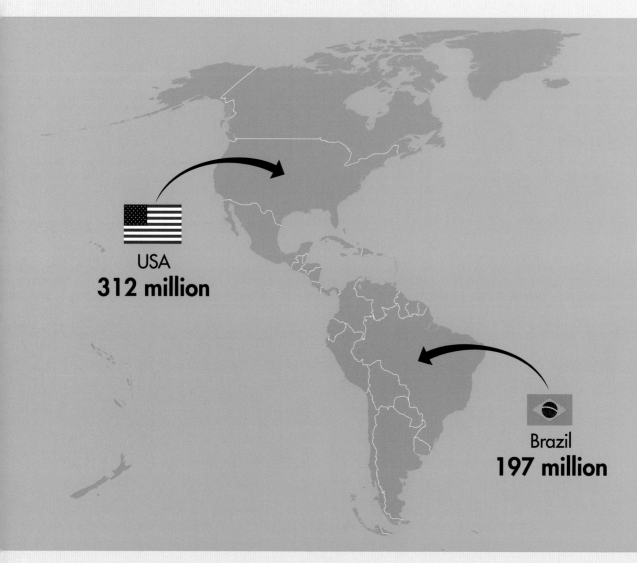

USA
312 million

Brazil
197 million

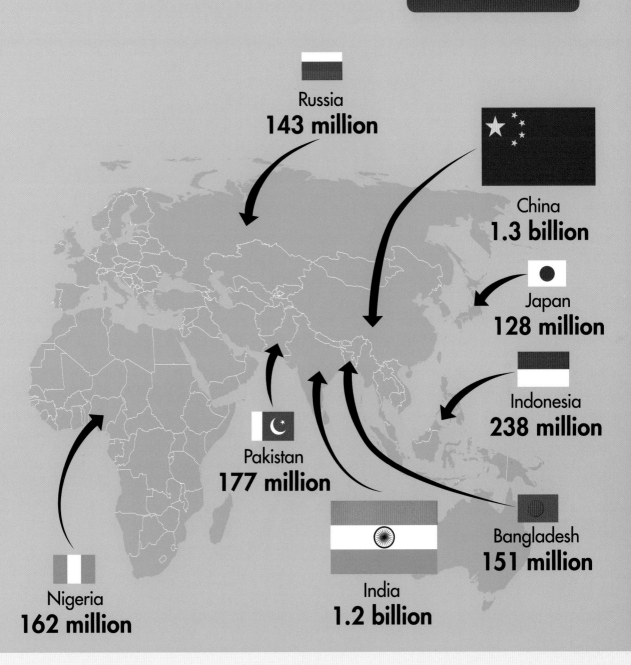

The sizes of the flags show how big the populations are.

Russia
143 million

China
1.3 billion

Japan
128 million

Indonesia
238 million

Pakistan
177 million

Bangladesh
151 million

Nigeria
162 million

India
1.2 billion

Growing countries

In some countries, the **population** is growing fast. This map shows some of the countries that are growing the fastest.

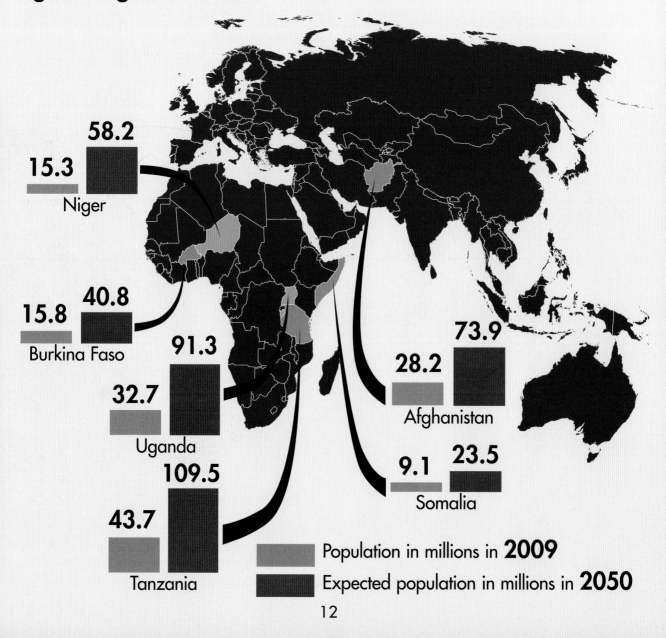

15.3
58.2
Niger

15.8
40.8
Burkina Faso

32.7
91.3
Uganda

43.7
109.5
Tanzania

28.2
73.9
Afghanistan

9.1
23.5
Somalia

Population in millions in **2009**

Expected population in millions in **2050**

Crowded countries and empty countries

Some countries are very crowded. Lots of people are squeezed into a small area. We say they are densely populated. This map shows the most densely populated countries.

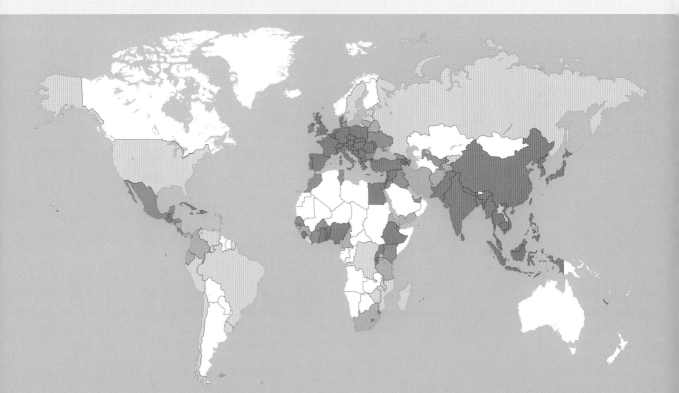

■ Most densely populated countries
□ Least densely populated countries

The biggest cities

This map shows the ten cities in the world that have the biggest **populations**. The data comes from the **United Nations**.

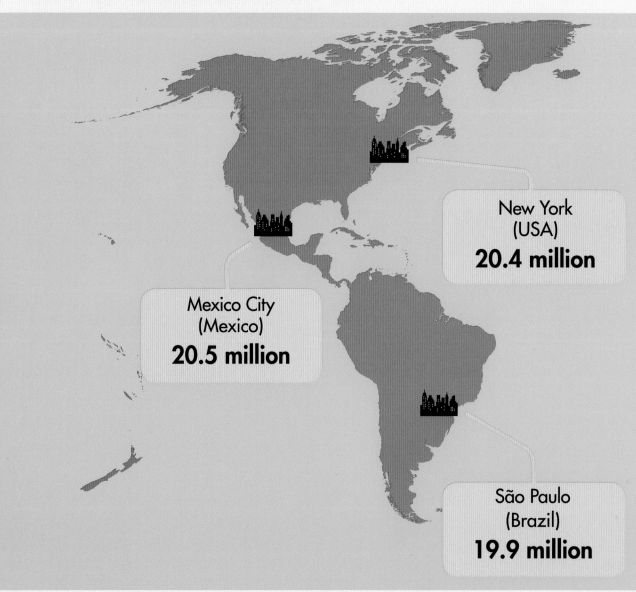

New York
(USA)
20.4 million

Mexico City
(Mexico)
20.5 million

São Paulo
(Brazil)
19.9 million

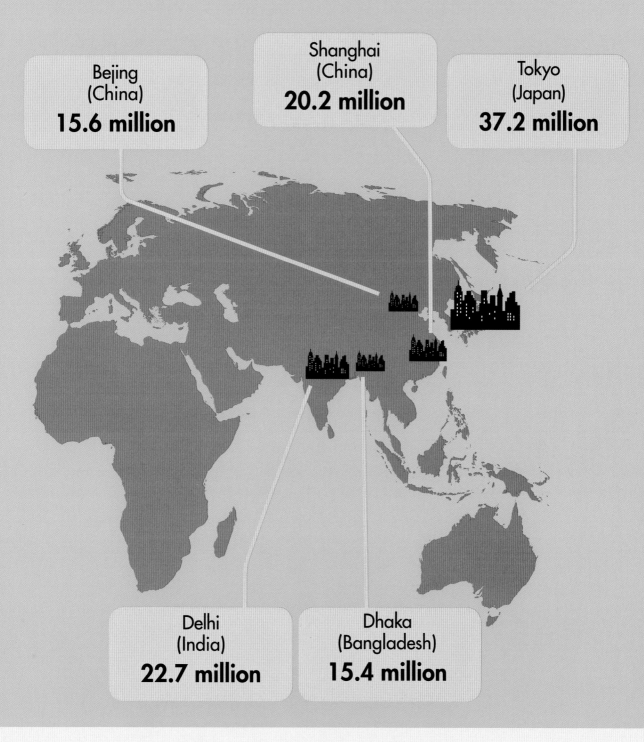

Bejing
(China)
15.6 million

Shanghai
(China)
20.2 million

Tokyo
(Japan)
37.2 million

Delhi
(India)
22.7 million

Dhaka
(Bangladesh)
15.4 million

Cities growing up

This graph shows how the **populations** of New York and London grew from 1800 until 2010. These huge cities started out as tiny villages.

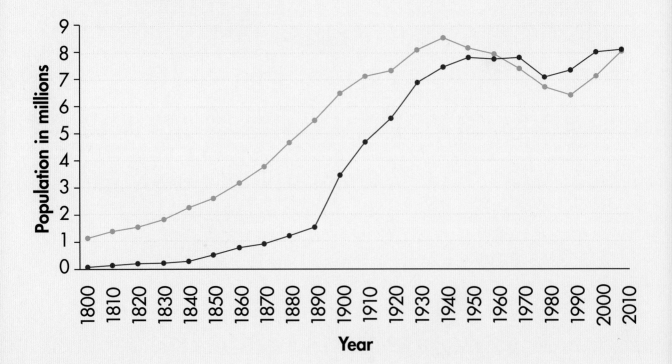

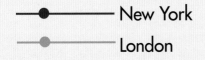

How big in the future?

As the world's populations grow, the world's cities will grow too. This chart shows how quickly the city of Lagos in Nigeria might grow in the future.

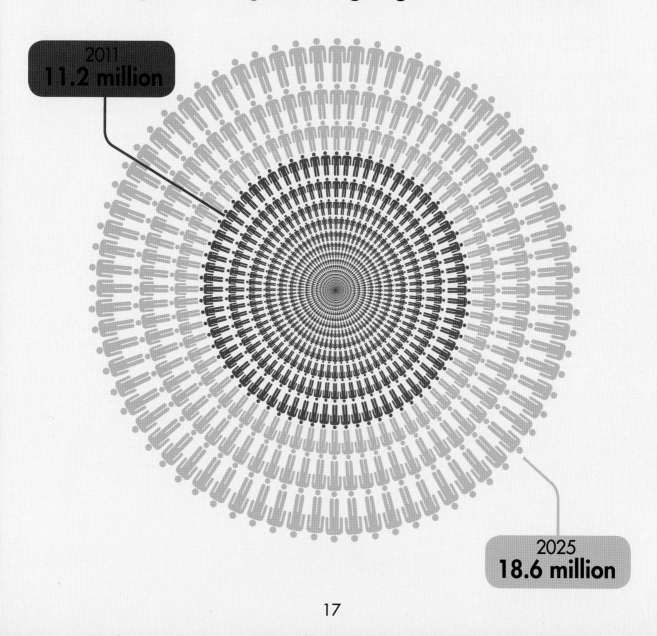

2011
11.2 million

2025
18.6 million

GENDER, AGE, AND LIFE EXPECTANCY

Men and women in the world

This infographic shows that there are almost the same number of males (men and boys) in the world as there are females (women and girls).

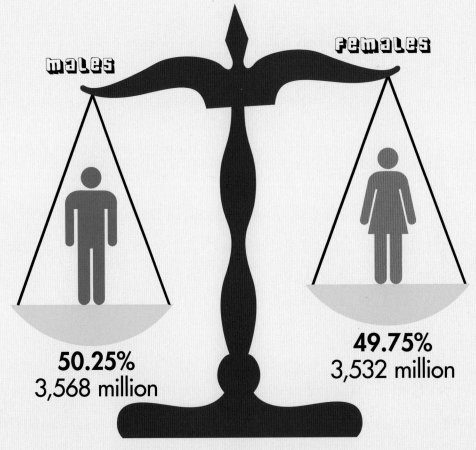

MALES

FEMALES

50.25%
3,568 million

49.75%
3,532 million

How old are people?

This chart shows how many young, middle-aged, and older people there are in the **population** of the United States.

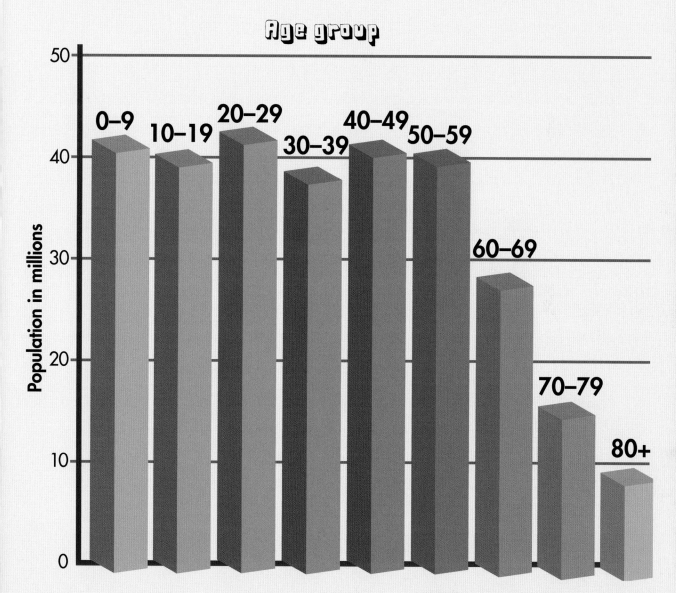

Age group

Population in millions

0–9 10–19 20–29 30–39 40–49 50–59 60–69 70–79 80+

50
40
30
20
10
0

Children and adults

This map shows you how many adults and how many children there are in each continent.

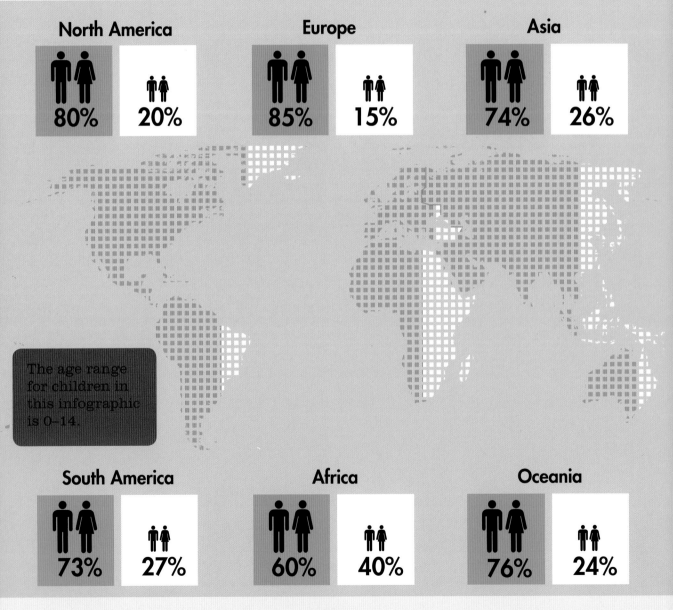

North America
80% 20%

Europe
85% 15%

Asia
74% 26%

The age range for children in this infographic is 0–14.

South America
73% 27%

Africa
60% 40%

Oceania
76% 24%

How long people live

This chart shows you how many years people live for (called life expectancy) in the United States and the United Kingdom.

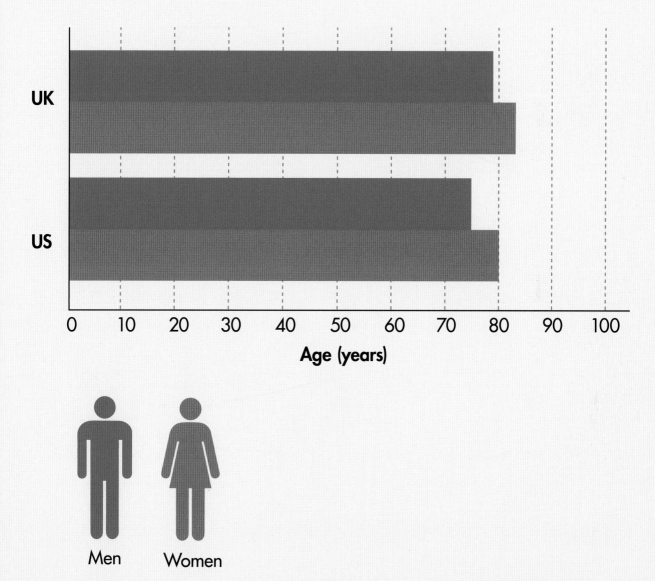

Age (years)

Men   Women

The longest and shortest lives

This map shows the countries where people live the longest lives and the shortest lives.

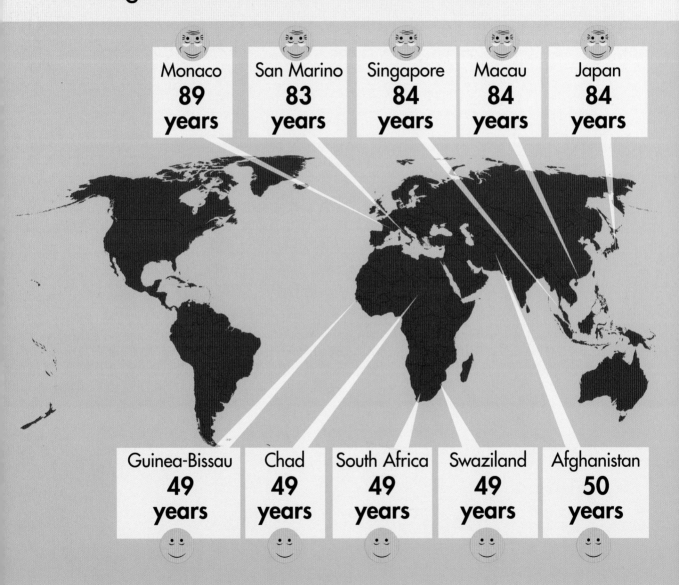

Monaco
89
years

San Marino
83
years

Singapore
84
years

Macau
84
years

Japan
84
years

Guinea-Bissau
49
years

Chad
49
years

South Africa
49
years

Swaziland
49
years

Afghanistan
50
years

Living for longer

How long people normally live for is called their life expectancy. This infographic shows how life expectancy has changed in the United Kingdom since 1900. Life expectancy is improving because medicine is getting better.

1900
49 years
45 years

1925
60 years
56 years

1950
70 years
65 years

1975
75 years
70 years

2013
82 years
77 years

LANGUAGE AND WRITING

Most common languages

People around the world speak hundreds of different languages. This infographic shows which languages are most commonly spoken.

Mandarin Chinese **12.4%**

Spanish **4.8%**

English **4.8%**

Arabic **3.3%**

Hindi **2.7%**

Bengali **2.7%**

Portuguese **2.6%**

Russian **2.1%**

Japanese **1.8%**

Standard German **1.3%**

Figures are shown as a percentage of the global **population**.

Reading and writing

In some countries, nearly everyone can read and write. In other countries, there are many people who can't read and write. This bar chart shows how many people can read and write in different countries.

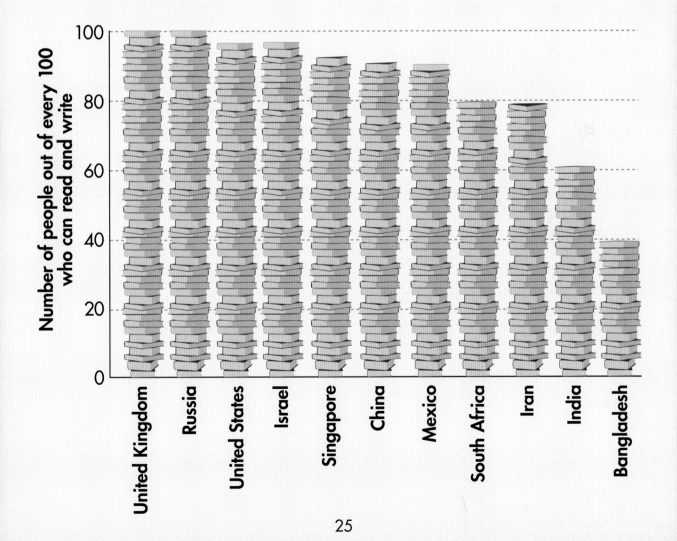

ETHNIC GROUPS

In many countries, the people come from a mixture of **ethnic groups**. These **pie charts** show the ethnic groups of the people who live in the United States, England and Wales, and Australia.

United States

White
75.1%

Black **12.3%**

American Indian and Alaska Native **0.9%**

Asian **3.6%**

Mixed race **2.4%**

Native Hawaiian and other Pacific Islander **5.6%**

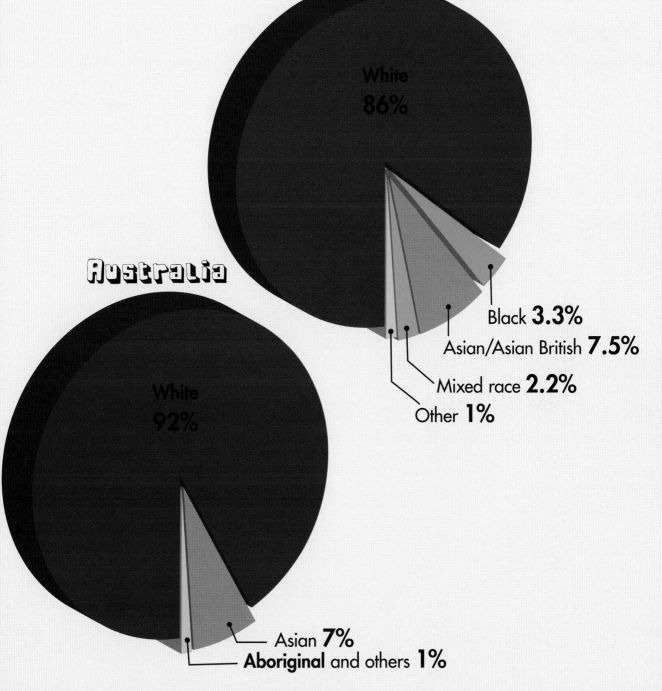

England and Wales

White 86%

Black **3.3%**
Asian/Asian British **7.5%**
Mixed race **2.2%**
Other **1%**

Australia

White 92%

Asian **7%**
Aboriginal and others **1%**

RELIGION AND BELIEF

Most popular religions

There are many different religions in the world. Some are more popular than others. This **pie chart** shows the most popular religions in the world.

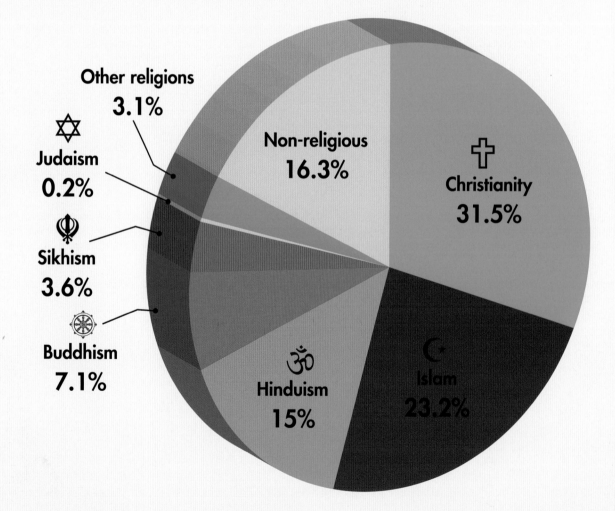

Other religions
3.1%

Judaism
0.2%

Sikhism
3.6%

Buddhism
7.1%

Non-religious
16.3%

Christianity
31.5%

Hinduism
15%

Islam
23.2%

Popular religions

This bar chart shows the most popular religions in the United States and England and Wales.

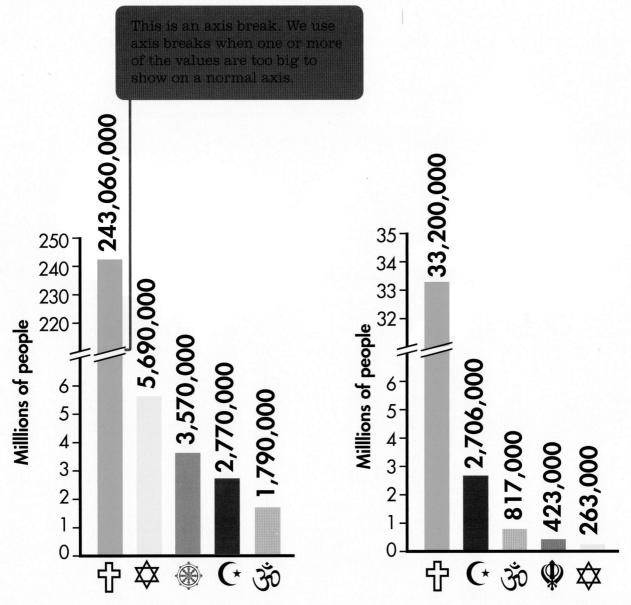

This is an axis break. We use axis breaks when one or more of the values are too big to show on a normal axis.

GLOSSARY

Aboriginal person who belongs to the native people of Australia

billion number that is equal to one thousand times one million; 1,000,000,000

ethnic group group of people of the same race or nationality

mixed race describes someone with ancestors from two or more different ethnic groups

pie chart circular chart that shows how something is divided up by showing pieces of a pie

population people who live in a place; number of people who live in a place

United Nations international organisation made up of most of the countries in the world

FIND OUT MORE

Books

Collins Primary World Atlas (Collins, 2013)

Earth's Growing Population (Headline Issues), Catherine Chambers (Heinemann Library, 2010)

Making Graphs (series), Vijaya Khisty Bodach (Capstone Press, 2008)

Websites

www.worldometers.info/world-population
You can find counters that estimate the world's population on this website.

nces.ed.gov/nceskids/createagraph/default.aspx
Visit this website to create your own graphs and charts.

INDEX